Welcome Baby

BY WELLERAN POLTARNEES

LAUGHING ELEPHANT

ISBN 1-59583-001-4

FIRST PRINTING   PRINTED IN CHINA THROUGH COLORCRAFT LTD., HONG KONG   ALL RIGHTS RESERVED

LAUGHING ELEPHANT BOOKS

3645 INTERLAKE AVENUE NORTH   SEATTLE   WASHINGTON   98103

WWW.LAUGHINGELEPHANT.COM

We welcome you baby and offer these wishes for the wonderful life ahead of you.

Your father welcomes you
with the joy of long anticipation.

Your mother welcomes you with great love,
for you are the long awaited reward
for her patience and care.

Your home will be a place of peace and caring nurture,

And your bed a small world of comfort and delight.

You will have uncountable good times,

And many friends to share them,

Including gentle animals.

You will see and love this world in all its variety
and beauty.

The sun and moon will continually
bless your life.

Days will hold you in their brightness,
and night enfold you in its peace.

You will have many lovely nights of sleep.

And many joyful awakenings.

Baby – we send you all of our love, and welcome you
to a glorious life.

Picture Credits